hers

hers

design with a feminine touch

Jacqueline deMontravel

Photographs by Marisa Crawford, Jacqueline deMontravel,
Bret Gum, Jaimee Itagaki, and Mark Tanner

Clarkson Potter/Publishers
New York

All rights reserved.
Published in the United States by Clarkson Potter/Publishers, an imprint of the Crown Publishing
Group, a division of Random House, Inc., New York.
www.crownpublishing.com
www.clarksonpotter.com

CLARKSON POTTER is a trademark and POTTER with colophon is a registered trademark of
Random House, Inc.

Library of Congress Cataloging-in-Publication Data
deMontravel, Jacqueline.
Hers : design with a feminine touch / Jacqueline deMontravel. — 1st ed.
p.   cm.
1. Interior decoration—Psychological aspects.   I. Romantic homes.
II. Title.   III. Title: design with a feminine touch.
NK2113.D46   2011
747.082—dc22   2011002263

ISBN 978-0-307-88598-2

Printed in China

Book design by Amy Sly
Book photographs by Marisa Crawford, Jacqueline deMontravel,
Bret Gum, Jaimee Itagaki, and Mark Tanner
Jacket design by Amy Sly
Jacket (front) photograph by Jacqueline deMontravel

1   3   5   7   9   10   8   6   4   2

First Edition

To
Adeline, Brielle & Olivia,
three young ladies
in the making

Introduction

Imagine a room where you can light as many candles as you want without worrying about fire hazards, or listen to cheesy music while reading the kind of gossip magazines that are usually relegated to grocery-store lines. Whether you are single or a married mother of four, to create a room where you have no one to answer to is a mission worth accepting.

Why did we let the boudoir go the way of the butler's pantry and the parlor room? Surely a woman's private space hasn't become obsolete. After all, a common trait in the female makeup is her need for her own place where she can be surrounded by pretty things that soothe her.

The origin of the boudoir is reflected in its name. In French, *bouder* means to sulk. Thus when a woman was experiencing the onset of a meltdown she would withdraw to her boudoir to unleash her emotions. Civilized and girly, *n'est-ce pas*? It is no wonder that the first boudoirs belonged to the mistresses of Louis XIV, as these ladies were unapologetically feminine and felt at ease in a room that promoted seduction.

The boudoir evolved into a place where a woman could be fussed over, have a quiet meal, entertain special guests, bathe and dress—in short, a place to just be feminine. The modern woman still needs this luxury, in the same way that a man needs his time in the garage. In today's world, alas, extra rooms are indulgences, given that no home ever has enough space.

So how do you create your own private space, especially when your kitchen doubles as the laundry room? It takes some imagination, some rethinking of your home's layout, and a little purging, but when that room is in place it can be life-altering.

Get into the spirit of decorating your space in the same manner you would when putting together a look for a black-tie event. You want to dazzle while being comfortable enough to last through a long, memorable night. You begin with your go-to dress, one that makes you feel beautiful and sexy. You then consider jewelry, shoes, and makeup. Think of your room as the dress, the accents as your accessories, and the color as your makeup.

A lanyard of tiny, white-colored shells lends a quiet note of the sea and adds a novel element to a bed's canopy. [above] An overlooked corner can become a favorite nook when designed with a handsome chair and go-to accessories, such as a throw, flowers, and great art. [opposite]

A room should captivate while being inviting; it should not only be comfortable but also make you feel at your best. Any lady worth her glamour knows that she must feel relaxed. It's a state of mind that comes from a secure place. Function, comfort, and style are a powerful triumvirate in achieving one's optimum space.

Decide on a look that you love, such as vintage, French Provincial, mid-century modern, or any other style that turns your space into a personal retreat. Whether you live in a three-bedroom cottage or in a one-window studio, you can achieve any look and mood with the clever use of paint, textiles, and accessories. Patterns and color combinations can also create an exquisite effect without becoming overpowering or outdated.

To keep the room's modern steel-gray walls from looking too cavernous, a bedside table and a tufted headboard in a contrasting light shade soften the look. The tabletop features well-appointed accessories, while the mirror brings in more light and glamour.

Decorators from Elsie de Wolfe to Celerie Kemble have used floral and chintz for traditional looks in a woman's space, but there is also a modern interpretation to the feminine side. Rather than ruffles and lace, a British West Indies or soothing beach vibe might be just the look to make your nook feel luxurious to you. In fact, throughout this book, you'll find a wide variety of feminine styles—from the completely girly to more restrained looks for those needing to accommodate male guests or family members. These spaces still serve as luxe retreats for the lady of the house, but in case you crave more feminine fantasy, look for the "Make It About Her" boxes for hints, tricks, and details for tweaking these spaces to your fancy.

When deciding where to create your favorite space in your home, a natural place to address is the bedroom. Rather than viewing this room as merely functional, see it as an opportunity to create an environment in which you can spend personal time napping, reading, primping, and losing yourself in those other pastimes that have become luxuries in our modern world.

> "It is the personality of the mistress that the home expresses. Men are forever guests in our homes, no matter how much happiness they may find there."
>
> —ELSIE DE WOLFE

As you get started, draw upon a variety of styles and inspirations to see how a bedroom can be more than a place of mad departures and much-needed sleep. Take inspiration from books, magazines, decorator show houses, travel, or the set design of an artful film to find a great look for your personal room.

A neglected space elsewhere in your home can be reinvented as your own. A sitting area that gets limited use can become your go-to spot if you cleverly rearrange what you already

A consortium of vintage finds creates a cozy, one-of-a-kind setting in this outdoor corner. **[opposite]** Vintage cottage elements—the time-worn distressed furnishings and classic rose pattern—are reminiscent of a great manor home. **[above]**

own and add a few well-appointed accents such as pictures or books. A beloved chair that is artfully positioned can be the spot you sink into with a book or your laptop. Even your kitchen table can become your favorite spot for drinking tea and writing letters.

Today's woman will be completely undone if she doesn't have a place in which to create. And there is no such thing as downtime when you can connect to the Web. Thus an environment in which to channel your creative outlets may be your ultimate retreat. From a small nook that was once a closet to a corner in the living room, a workspace can be more fabulous than functional. And don't forget the inspiration board: a display of photos, swatches, color samples, and other items that you find soothing or thought-provoking. Losing yourself in nostalgia and reflection can allow some of your best ideas to come to life.

If you're an outdoor enthusiast, create a personal space en plein air simply by adding a vase of flowers, throws, architectural elements, and comfortable items more typically associated with the interior. With such a cozy design you're bound to find yourself enjoying morning coffee or dinners alfresco more often.

Essentially any space can be viewed as an opportunity to cultivate a haven. And in this book you'll find creative ways to carve out your retreat anywhere in the home. Reexamine your rooms' current functions, clear the clutter, and find creative storage solutions. Don't have the space? Add dimension to your existing rooms, transform your bedroom into a sanctuary, or tap into your creative side to design a room you'll always want to come home to.

How do you make your nook sexy? A place where a man will feel at home as well? Items ranging from a mini fridge stocked with favorite edibles to a music system to a simple bar trolley will make this the place where guests will also want to be.

Personal space is as necessary as air and water. Today's busy lives find people in a constant swirl of interaction, following rules of conduct. Downtime is a luxury and, unfortunately, having a moment to primp comes in at number thirty-two on a daily to-do list. All women love to play dress-up. We are at our best when we feel pretty and can relax in an environment that nurtures our femininity. Every woman deserves one place that is unapologetically *hers*. With a style that defines her. Where she sets the rules.

There are many pieces that come together to make a home office a more enjoyable place. This green desk is detailed with gilded trim, which complements the desk accessories and brass chair. The shelves are not only functional but also an opportunity to group collections and favorite books.

Bed Time

Your bedroom is the most obvious choice for creating a retreat, as it doesn't get more private than this. From those days when you just don't want to get out of bed to the weeks you'd like to have end on Tuesday, an inviting room adds good reason to slip into seclusion. A successful bedroom should relax, soothe, and reinvigorate its occupant. The original French boudoir was intended for a woman to gather herself when she was feeling out of sorts. She could partake of those activities that made her feel at her best, such as crafting, primping, or entertaining guests by invitation. Today such a room offers a simpler and more pleasurable experience than time clocked on a therapist's couch.

Build a room around one great piece, such as a well-dressed bed. Correlating colors unify the furnishings and accessories in this ultra-feminine vignette. When accessorizing with white, any size or style will do justice to the color's soft neutrality. You can layer on as many pillows and textures, such as a crocheted quilt and gauzy canopy, for a comfortable, romantic feel.

Begin by tapping into a style that inspires you. There are many enchanting looks you can achieve without making your bedroom nirvana look overly girly. Candles, pillows that appear to be pulled from your lingerie drawer, feathered slippers, and soft lighting one would expect in a bordello are obviously feminine but may be more threatening to a budding romance than talks of wedding venues or ex-boyfriends. Considering the variety of design trends to choose from, including Swedish Gustavian, French Provincial, vintage, and British Colonial, any look that stimulates your passions and makes you feel beautiful can become the theme that sets the tone for your bedroom.

Every awe-inducing bedroom blends a poetic mix of color, texture, and personal memorabilia—the accent pieces that reveal clues to its dweller's interests. Consider preparing your space for its reinvention by giving it a fresh coat of paint, replacing old carpeting with wood flooring, cleaning the windows, and taking measurements if window treatments are part of the redesign.

make adjustments

Examine your room's layout. A simple adjustment, such as moving your bed closer to a wall, may carve out a nook for a reading chair or a dressing space. Edit out furnishings that have no function to create more room for your intended needs. If your bedside only calls for a water glass and reading material, a small bedside table will suffice. Or perhaps move your bureau beside your bed to double as a table and storage.

Classic pieces with ornate trimming set the theme. Add like-minded decorative pieces for more color and femininity.

This room takes a playful turn through pillows, artwork, and a quilt that are as colorful as a Japanese cartoon. To keep bright colors from looking garish, choose one dominant color, such as hot pink, and weave in items in contrasting colors, such as those that are echoed in the quilt.

hunt for ideas

Read magazines and design books and shop for ideas until you have settled on a look that's totally you. Consider what you already own, edit carefully, and then add new pieces. Go to the limit: Dress your bed in layers of linens. Decorate your walls with artwork that was previously used in more formal rooms, such as oils, fine prints, or exuberant pictures of romantic imagery. Pull in warm notes such as rugs, lamps, and a chair you could fall asleep in. Push the details even further with stacks of books placed here and there, candles, flowers, and personalized collections.

consider color

Color sets any room's direction, but it is especially important in the bedroom, which is typically a small space. A white room is bright and expansive. White also acts as a blank canvas on which furnishings and accessories set the theme. As an example, dark furnishings paired with accent pieces and linens in blue and white create a British Colonial look. Add a zebra-print rug, and you have instant glamour. A mirrored bedside table speaks romance. Just a few bold accessories placed against a neutral background can have great impact. Experiment with color by testing out gutsy designs through unexpected colors, perhaps easing into a scheme with your bedding or a headboard, for a modern interpretation. Step it up even further by painting a wall in an earth tone or in a whimsical color you thought only belonged in a Crayola box.

Color can also be feminine without scaring off the opposite sex. Pale pink can be neutralized with dark wood or touches of black. Soft grays and light blues are not just for boys' rooms but are calming and nurturing for all. Due to their lightness, such shades are more subtle than sassy pink or cheery yellow without being too gender-neutral.

details, details

A woman's bedroom should provide a sensual experience, an opportunity to include soft linens, fabrics, and throws. Layer a mix of patterns that share a color or a print theme through bed linens, the rug, an upholstered chair, or window treatments. Or choose an all-white scheme that soothes. White is a versatile color that need not look sterile. Varying the tone through linens and silvery accessories helps produce an ethereal effect.

An assortment of pillows, from Euro shams to a delicate neck roll, is the kind of detail that reflects a thoughtfully designed bedroom where leisure and daydreaming can occur. Pillows and throws are also "migratory" and can be moved from chair to bed according to your relaxation needs.

Consider ways to extend soft fabrics beyond your bed and furnishings. Tack a block of fabric on the wall above your bed, framed by crown molding you can purchase at any home-supply store, for an original headboard. In a neutral room you can be as creative as you wish with your headboard's design, which is an opportunity to showcase an eye-catching statement piece.

Susan Ellison's bedroom is a contrast between light and dark and masculine and feminine. The proprietress of the linens store Blue Springs Home, she has a shopkeeper's intuition that shows through her use of fabrics and linens. Textiles change the mood of a room and warm it up, especially during a change of season. "And always add some fresh flowers," adds Susan, to bring in an extra dose of color and a natural element.

This French enamel remembrance plaque adds interest to a beautifully framed mirror with its unusual composition. Setting a mirror across from the bed brings in light, space, and beauty. **[above left]** Delicate belts are displayed beautifully on a bedside table, another example of fashionable accessories lending their appeal to a room's vignette. **[above center]** Something as simple as neatly arranged note cards can unify a room's theme. **[above right]**

accessorize

To finish your bedroom's design, apply the same principles you use when dressing. Any accessory should increase the oomph factor of a style without overpowering the look. Using your accessories and favorite finds to bring in your personality will make the space even more meaningful.

Once you establish the look you want to create, consider the complementary accents that draw you in. Glass jars filled with shells evoke simplicity and calm. A colorful stack of quality note cards in a Lucite box is both elegant and playful. True collectors treat their possessions with high esteem and are on the lookout in shops, at flea markets, and at online auctions for treasures to add to their lair. Control your collection's look by displaying it on bookshelves, in vitrines, or on tabletops in attractive groupings. Emphasize each item's color and pattern so the whole collection

A chaise longue artfully arranged diagonally near a window creates a cozy nook in a generously sized bedroom. Small details such as the pillow, throw, and candle answer the occupant's needs for an entire afternoon.

can contribute to your room's overall theme. Group items that share a theme, color, or texture. Place the taller pieces in the back and winnow down to smaller collectibles. Or try a skyline effect. Regardless, the design is a gradual process that allows you to add to and subtract from what's there.

To keep your look clean rather than live in a scrapbook of a room, continually catalog your inventory and shelve those items that are interfering with a room's natural balance. Fewer items thoughtfully displayed

are more calming to the eye than a mishmash of items competing for a limited display area.

While an open space becomes an invitation to place accessories, keep a few general rules in mind. For example, consider scale. A tall, clunky item on a skinny bedside table will look like a skyscraper on a five-mile island. A small space should accommodate small items, while larger spaces are suited to grander items such as stacks of photography books and lamps.

Small rugs are low-maintenance and can warm up a space or add just the right amount of color or pattern to pull together a theme. Mirrors are a common design feature that add an instant luxurious touch, giving depth to a room while providing a place to primp. Art is what makes a room distinctive. When hanging artwork, do not place it higher than five to eight inches above a bed's headboard. Group pictures so they all form a clean grid, even if the frames differ in size. Two small square pictures can be stacked beside a long vertical one to create an even look.

get personal

The most inviting rooms need not have designer fingerprints. In fact, rooms that best reveal their residents often show the most character. A space that provides insight into your interests and passions becomes a deeper, more enriching place, one that you—and any guests lucky enough to be welcomed—will want to linger in.

Take inspiration from rooms you find luxurious and spin it to your taste. Grand window treatments, a quiet sitting area, a family of pillows on a bed that could lull an insomniac to sleep are all luxurious details that can be tailored to your needs and to the amount of space you have to work with. Then add pieces

"Luxury must be comfortable, otherwise it is not luxury."

—COCO CHANEL

of your personal history, such as photographs, books, collectibles, and keepsakes. Typically, things that tug on a memory provide beauty while keeping the moment in perpetuity. Says Lizabeth McGraw of Tumbleweed & Dandelion, "We all feel feminine in a space filled with white linen and comfy cushions. Layer the room with natural soy-based candles, soothing lighting, and small touches such as favorite pictures and travel mementos. I love to leave special postcards in books that I might pick up now and again. It always warms my heart to come upon a memory."

The pieces you choose for your home provide comfort, whether through beauty or a personal story, and therefore become the touchstones in the ultimate personal space. However natural it is to want to include all your belongings in your vignettes, if an item does not blend into your environment, reconsider its placement. "You must find everything in your home to be pleasing to your eye. If it doesn't meet this litmus test, it must go," says Kathleen Delgado of Vintageweave Interiors.

a case for a canopy

A bed draped with a canopy sets off a fury of excitement. Night can't arrive too soon. It's like having high tea at a storied hotel: You must dress the part. You feel fancy. Ladies who have beds with canopies wear furry slippers and robes with lacy trim. Something as simple as a gauzy sheet secured with an elaborate crown is a simple way to achieve a romatic look. Canopies can be added to any bed and used with any style. When a bed is covered with a canopy, sleep is a special occasion each night.

Monogrammed pillows are one of the most effective and time-honored ways to personalize a bed. Gold accessories on the wall add symmetry.

The reliable parts to complete this make-believe setting include a crystal chandelier, a stylized canopy, layered shades, pink ruffled pillows, and china plates hung on the wall. Who says a woman can't still feel like a princess? **[above left]** Food and tea taste better when beautifully presented. The iconic numbers bring this romantic look into the modern day. **[above right]**

gadget-free zone

Imagine taking a week off from telephones and e-mail. The results may be as dramatic as a Balinese spa holiday. It's a romantic notion worth trying to achieve. Consider limiting use of the computer and the phone in your bedroom. Remove the television. Such restrictions will lead you to indulge in calmer, more introspective pleasures such as perusing the untouched reading material that has been multiplying on your bedside table. For Lynn Goldfinger of Paris Hotel Boutique, her sanctuary is a place with no computer or electronics: "A place to walk away from my home-based job and just gaze out the window and look at the trees," she says. Until a week magically clears for island travel, make your bedroom the ultimate escape.

White distressed wood is a cornerstone of the romantic style. The paint and wall pieces set the look, while crisp white linens and a surplus of pillows provide a sense of calm and comfort. Symmetry is attained through the ornamented ceiling lamp and tray table, as well as through the color, which is echoed in the bench's upholstery, in the initials on the pillow, and in the artwork.

Pick a Style

We may live in the twenty-first century, but a bedroom can take inspiration from a variety of eras and locales, with a little of your femininity and personality in the mix.

British West Indies

Three colors dominate this dreamy, sophisticated look: dark chocolate, blue, and white. The style combines rich mahogany furnishings and dark wood floors, white painted walls, and linens and slipcovered chairs with blue and white accents such as printed bedding and porcelain.

Coastal

Souvenirs from the sea, light colors, and soft linens work well for homes that welcome sand in the house; a beach look takes you to your favorite summer holiday any time of the year. Play on the colors of the beach to keep the look light and feminine. Add soft touches such as gauzy window treatments, pillows, and linens.

Ethnic-inspired

Orange, magenta, purple, and the brightest hues on the color wheel are found in fabrics with prints you could get lost in. Ethnic-inspired design takes you to faraway places like Morocco, India, and Asia. Weave in accents acquired on your most exotic travels, like jeweled boxes and shimmery lanterns, or just a few overseas items picked up from a visit on eBay.

French

An abundance of heavy textiles, motley furnishings, and pieces that have been used in past times pays homage to the fuss-free French country life. The look is not precise, though it never looks cluttered, with a variety of timeworn necessities such as crystal and silver always being put to use.

Gustavian

This clean Swedish design focuses on quality pieces and soothing colors such as soft gray, blue, or green reminiscent of a seascape. Gustavian interiors can be classical, contemporary, or country in tone, though the look maintains a light design through pillows, upholstery, and furnishings that show their patina. The clean lines and colors are soothing and feminine, which steadies the focus on beautiful things.

Mid-century

This style calls upon the indulgent martini lunch, shorthand on steno pads, and furniture created in shapes that look like punctuation marks and that evoke a more sophisticated time. Mid-century is very today with its clean, organic designs that focus on quality pieces.

Romantic

With soft colors, layers of linens, and accessories that play up the fun of being a girl, the romantic style is overtly girly. No detail should be underplayed. Call upon your prettiest accessories, such as pillows and candles, by the dozen, as an excess of gorgeous items spawns romance. A man will appreciate the "woman's touch" and the effort made.

Traditional

A trip to the manor house gets toned down for today's lifestyle. Four-poster beds, a stack of books color-coded by binding, Oriental rugs, and rich colors and texture give the look as much warmth as a hungry fire.

hamptons–british west indies

connection It is fitting that this bedroom overlooks the Pacific. Ocean views are stiff competition for a room's design, but the owner, Susie Mitchell, managed to capitalize on her home's greatest asset. Drawing inspiration from the British West Indies and the Hamptons, she uses a contrast of dark wood and white, peppered with "collections of sea nature and the color blue." **[previous pages]**

indigo blues For an updated take on classic blue and white, Susie Mitchell of the interior design firm Hearts Desire had pillows and throws made from vintage indigo-blue textiles that a local artist created. **[above]**

get in line Blue pinstripes are not just meant for Ivy League fraternity attire: The look is timeless. Here, the duvet covers set the room's tone, which is continued through the worn picture frames and grain-sack headboards created by designer Loretta Kilheffer. The soft blues are reminiscent of the ocean, and shell art and pictures are the natural accent. The use of twin beds keeps guests in mind, but in the meantime the quiet tailored look is still the perfect escape when the master bedroom simply won't do. **[opposite]**

study the classics

Rich furnishings and textures that you would expect to find in a Scottish bed-and-breakfast create a warm retreat. This bedroom brings in such traditional accessories as window treatments and bedding in woodland colors and prints. An oversized portrait becomes the ideal statement piece for leaning atop the mantel—no hanging required. An assortment of flower arrangements pulls the room into the present day while adding a natural element. **[opposite]**

best seat in the house

A stately chair gets a new life with fresh paint and upholstery in an unexpected coral toile. A simple landscape painting is a delicate, one-of-a-kind detail, while personal items thoughtfully arranged on the table lend personality and style. **[above]**

Make It About Her
Swapping the autumnal colors and patterns for lighter pastels and florals will make over the space and bring a younger energy to the room.

Make It About Her
Bring in textural elements, such as a cashmere throw and a small pillow, for warmer notes and a sense of leisure.

dark and light Pale blue walls and chair upholstery are at one with the dark chocolate bed and dresser. The tropical ceiling fan with banana leaf–shaped blades and a soft curtain on the canopy evoke the romance of a tropical getaway. **[above]**

give it some thought Investment pieces, such as a bed with exquisite bamboo detailing, will forever give a room a styled look. A harmonious flow is in motion from the soft Indian block-print pillows and delicate wall art. Any curious visitor will be won over by the grouping of photographs on the bureau. **[opposite]**

Baroness Monica von Neumann on "Boudoir Neglect"

The bedroom is the one place we neglect the most, but it is a retreat from all that you have endured through the course of your day. Its function is to soothe, so treat it as the proverbial slippers and cocktail and dress it to the nines. Avoid "boudoir neglect" with the following tips:

- A nightstand is imperative, even if you only have one. However, if you have the space, flanking the bed with nightstands may make the room appear more balanced.

- Add a bit of glam in subtle ways, whether it's with your duvet cover, picture frames (for special family photos), or a nice area rug (very helpful for framing a bed).

- Invest in a down comforter. If you are allergic to down, choose one of the many fabulous hypoallergenic alternatives.

- Hang artwork in the bedroom to create a feeling of peace and tranquillity and to add warmth to the space. Bare walls are unattractive, even if you are a minimalist. Pick art that makes you happy and highlights your personal style and taste, whether it be impressionist, pop art, or contemporary. In addition to paintings, consider drawings, lithographs, photographs, and sculptures.

- Decorating with vases, in any size or color, brings a pop of color and interest to your dresser, nightstand, or vanity.

- Splurge on sheets with a high thread count; they are so soft and luxurious. It's an investment you won't regret.

- The right mix of pillows is essential to creating an atmosphere—although how many is negotiable.

- Always have two or three (minimum) oversized Euro pillows dressed in shams. Euro pillows make the bed look more luxurious, balance the other pillows, and add fullness to the bed. If you have a wooden headboard (rather than a padded one), they will definitely add comfort for lounging.

- Add one set of standard or king shams depending on the size of your bed. A proper bed should have four pillows in addition to the Euros.

Choose decorative pillows depending on your taste, whether you're traditional, whimsical, or modern.

- Always have at least one pillow that displays your design aesthetic or personality (I have a poodle pillow, a body lumbar pillow, and a sequined pillow). A throw blanket is a thoughtful addition to your bed for napping on a whim without messing up the covers. It can also be very useful in pulling a theme together.

- Bed skirts are lovely, and they can be either modern or traditional depending on personal taste. Look for styles that are box stitched, pleated, or simply loose, any of which gives a finishing touch to the overall look. Who wants to look at furniture legs or under the bed anyway?

In Baroness Monica von Neumann's Hollywood home, a Zen bed anchors the corner nook with prime views of the outdoors. All soothing touches are in operation, such as flowers, candles, and warm textiles. Monica is a champion of creating a place that pacifies. She advocates that a bedroom should not be passed over, a common mistake she calls "boudoir neglect." [following pages]

a bold move Walls painted in a yellow and orange striped pattern you'd see on a Floridian rugby team's uniforms create the foundation of a spirited bedroom. The hand-made floral-patterned headboard adds a pretty, personal touch, while the linens are simplified to keep the look clean. **[opposite]**

get on board Headboards create a styled look without having to be an exorbitant expense. Here, designer Natalie Umbert found a paper she liked, which she framed within decorative wall molding found at any home improvement store. **[above]**

cartoon character Design a room around personal collectibles and interests. In this bedroom, the wall color complements Mickey Mouse, cartoon strips, and pop culture. Geometric patterns lend themselves to accent pieces such as the rug, pillows, and lampshades. The variety of patterns is unified with a classic red and black color scheme and favored belongings are tamed with efficient shelving. This eight-compartment piece neatly stores books and personal keepsakes while revealing the resident's personal style. **[opposite]**

shady character Lampshades are an easy way to make a statement and establish a mood in a room and allow you to keep the harsh overhead light turned off. Pair them with accessories that share a color or a time period to complete the look. **[above left]**

famous groups Figurines as disparate as Buddhist icons and Mickey Mouse are linked harmoniously through color and texture. **[above right]**

pop in Step into a piece of pop art with a whimsical display of color, accessories, and gravity-defying dressers that can challenge the sea-wary. In this raw loft space, the resident has fun with shapes and color, right up to the throw blanket diagonally placed on the bed. **[opposite]**

major hang-up A grouping of artwork holds its own on charcoal walls. Splashes of vibrant color, such as Kelly green and red, add punch. **[above]**

modern classic Pink sheds its girly image with dark accents. Details such as the retro rugs, animal-print and toile pillows, and a black pendant chandelier relate to today's style while evoking the past. A mirror becomes a focal point thanks to its dramatic size and exceptional frame. A window seat is further primped with an overstuffed cushion. **[previous pages]**

read it in black and white Silhouettes are fantastic design pieces due to their classic design and simplicity. Framed against light pink they partake of one of the hottest color combinations that endures. The heavy borders on the window treatments and moldings play on the geometric scheme. **[above]**

pale pink is the new white With a shade of pink so light it's almost hard to detect its hue, you can design a space as if the walls were white. Such a color is feminine yet sophisticated enough not to dissuade a male visitor. A vibrant yellow bedspread becomes the focal point for a one-of-a-kind look. **[opposite]**

tree hugger This bedroom takes its cue from the view outside. A storied tree that stretches its branches across the window and the room's rooftop creates the feel of living in a tree house. "I selected pieces for the room that would foster that calm atmosphere," says designer Brooke Giannetti of her bedroom and, in doing so, she chose furnishings in a soft neutral palette. A potted tree tucked away in the corner and garden clippings parlay the charm found just outside. "Our bedroom is the perfect space to relax at the end or beginning of the day," she says.

gilded age Pieces with touches of gold are always a classic addition to a bedroom vignette. The color can add symmetry to a room's theme or hold its own in more neutral territory. **[above left]**

sweeping gestures For the grandest statement that will capture light and beauty, look to a trumeau mirror, or pier glass. These mirrors have an illustrious past, as they were used above fireplaces in elegant European homes. Now they have become a dependable accessory in giving a room an assured dose of glamour. The silky window treatments echo other haute features within the room. **[above right]**

upon closer investigation

This deliciously tiny box has exquisite detailing and holds its own as the primary accent piece on a table. Displaying important pieces individually keeps the look clean while showing off their signature beauty. **[above left]**

complementing patterns

A variety of patterns on this bed blends seamlessly due to a shared color and theme. Buttressed by an upholstered headboard, the look is elegant and inviting. Colors of blue and taupe have just the right note of femininity without alienating the opposite sex. A combination of textures is used, such as cotton, satin, and velvet, which all appeal to a woman's sensuality. **[above right]**

fetching slippers

Small accessories have a big impact in a room with a clean landscape. These embroidered slippers offer a dazzling spot of color that immediately grabs the eye. **[right]**

like-minded group
Pale blue, mint green, and champagne tones unify this cinematic vignette. Elegant accessories play up the style and provide the ideal place for primping. Jewels and gold punctuate the clothes and fabrics, and the space becomes a setting for dressing up in an adult world. A floor-to-ceiling mirror completes the look as a statement piece that's integral to a dressing room.

ocean views Starfish, shells, and collections from the sea are calming bedroom accessories. They can be creatively arranged, such as in an elegant vessel or boxed frame, and will soften a look with their neutral tones. **[above]**

romantic age Antique pieces come together through color and texture. The bureau provides the perfect surface on which to display cherished accessories such as silver and reflective frames, a crystal pendant lamp, and a mirrored vanity tray holding favored pieces. An arrangement of garden-picked flowers adds the right jolt of color to the serene palette. **[opposite]**

black and blue marks

A classic black and blue color scheme recalls a more glamorous era. Playing on the sense of allure evoked by the palette, the celluloid look is reinforced through a mirrored bedside table and a button-tufted settee. The table's accessories include a playful mix of fashion books and an orbed lamp for a thoroughly modern sensibility. A vintage black-and-white fashion photo shares the same bold appeal as the Chanel book, which stands playfully upright. **[opposite]**

personal montage

For a glimpse of character that can be as revealing as a page in a diary, create a wall display featuring a mix of artistic and personal photographs. The grouping is less manic with the chunky black frames set against calming pale blue. Bookcases were organized with some favorite books arranged horizontally, others vertically, to maintain balance with the occasional keepsake positioned here and there. A black-and-white image of Audrey Hepburn gazing into the windows of Tiffany & Co. is the token piece of glam art. **[above]**

don't take things too seriously
This bedroom is an exercise in lively decorating. It becomes an open canvas with plenty of roominess from the bed's built-in drawers and multiple windows that allude to more space and render this a haven for natural light. The playful linens are anything but humdrum. **[above left]**

exclusive hideaway
A charming window seat in a bedroom takes on a more sophisticated feel through an arrangement of pillows in updated patterns. The addition of a mirror provides a window effect to create intrigue and expand the sense of space. Laying a faux-fur throw on the cushion contributes an easy touch of instant glamour. **[above right]**

my space
In this bedroom, my husband vamped up an awkward space by installing a built-in bed. The drawers beneath offer extra storage, while favorite photographs can be hung on the wall in lieu of lining up picture frames on a dresser. We added movable wall lamps to free up even more space. White distressed frames are works of art on their own and keep the look clutter-free due to the neutral shade. Considering that white dominates the room's scheme to create airiness, colorful pillowcases add the right punch of color. The skylight and leaded windows, designed by a local craftsman, bring in light and a one-of-a-kind look, while still allowing for private moments. **[opposite]**

connect four Susan Feldman, cofounder of the home décor site One Kings Lane, followed four principles to elevate her bedroom from a place of rest to a multipurpose room of relaxation. "Make sure there is a really comfortable chair to sit in; always have a beautiful cashmere throw; have a favorite candle nearby; and hang a great piece of art."

see the writing on the wall
On the bedside corner, Susan Feldman hung a piece of art with simple graphics. Another framed work leans on the end table to add insouciance. Susan deliberately chose artwork that expresses a theme of romance. These pieces serve as a visual love note for her husband to enjoy every day. **[left]**

fluff pieces
An extravagant use of pillows shows that comfort is held in high regard. All the prints share the same coloring and vintage theme, so they can be moved around. The bed need not be the only spot designated as comforting. **[below left]**

destination point
This tiny cottage shed shows the many charms of a single-wall-construction unit. With limited space, details abound, reinforcing a theme of beach life from decades ago. The distressed column and vintage floral painting are nostalgic pieces that evoke a summer vacation destination. **[below right]**

detail oriented

A brass bed, a bureau that shows its patina, and a handsomely upholstered chair are inviting with their vintage appeal. The accents are numerous, and the use of blue and red creates a consistent look.

Claim
Some Space

I f not in the bedroom, create another place in the home that is pure enchantment to you. Simplify the challenge by carving out a nook or corner of a room as your space. Determine the look based on styles that influence you. You may choose to mirror a childhood place. Or go for the exotic, channeling a look from that movie where the woman abandons her lonely life and finds a lover in a foreign land. Perhaps it is your interpretation of a single woman's New York apartment when wearing gloves to the office on summer days was the custom.

Clara DiGiuseppe, a design blogger and dealer, chose the prettiest shade of blue to transform this corner from a seating area to a favored place. Every chosen piece is simple in style and shade. Selected wall art is arranged in a tight grid topped by an architectural remnant in a unique shape that provides depth and interest to the wall. Clara's daughter drew the portrait of a ballerina, which adds warm sentiment.

Recall your most memorable experiences when visiting the home of a friend or family member to find the nostalgic details that will really make this space yours. Perhaps a candle was burning with an unforgettable scent, or a simple arrangement of flowers brightened a room, or snacks were served on gorgeous plates that once belonged to a close relative. Rich elements make others feel at ease, and perhaps take a conversation to a higher level. Music sounds better. A chair is more comfortable. Such details belong in the room of a woman who knows her way around the Left Bank. Even when you're decorating an appropriated space, it is this process of giving it a signature style that will make it your favorite retreat.

family obligations

Surround yourself with personal luxuries that soothe and you'll end up with a home that balances family life and your own. Brooke Giannetti of Velvet & Linen, a design and home furnishing store, is in the business of living practically but with style. The wife of an architect and mother of three with an around-the-clock business and a demanding home life, she knows how to create a personal retreat that's still based on family needs. "I think people are comfortable in our homes because they are filled with things that feel relaxed and comfortable," says Brooke. "Because I have a large family, I don't want spaces that feel untouchable. I am drawn to pieces that have a sense of age to them and that only get better with time and use. Even our pine floors get better looking as they show the dents and scuffs that have been added through the years."

Loretta Kilheffer of the home decor and furnishings company Full Bloom Cottage also brings her design sense into raising a family of three boys. "I believe you have to think about how you are going to use the

A wingback chair and a generously stuffed couch are far from frumpy with sharp colors and pillows in haute designs. An ottoman acts as a table while the wheels make it movable so that this room is adaptable. The room has a more intimate feel from the mocha tones in the furnishings and on the wall.

Janet Solomon, of FrenchBlue & Company, modulates light from the paneled curtains to achieve an ethereal glow, and her winged sculpture is an elegant representation of nature's art. [above left] Impressive design books paired with sea treasures become a signature look in creating a welcoming space. The coral and smooth white stones bring a down-to-earth quality to the vignette. [above right] "Art made from nature is always current and will be forevermore," Janet says. Souvenirs from the outdoors share a soft hue, texture, and style that bring feminine qualities to a favorite space. [opposite]

space, and for my living room with young boys, I knew that a slipcovered sectional was the only way to go. I wanted a room where everyone could gather and be comfortable. Once I had that in place, I filled the room with things I love; my antique ocean oil paintings and white coral are a staple for me. I searched for years for the perfect chippy antique mantel, which I think sets the tone for the whole living room."

Despite a household where the men outnumber the lady four to one, Loretta got her way with her beautiful things that are not so off-putting to the opposite sex. Her rooms are an exercise in how to bring feminine appeal into a modern home. Overly girly, with the gratuitous use of lace, florals, and pastels, is not the only version of a woman's well-appointed room. We love pretty things artfully arranged, pieces with history and romance, and with these we can create a room that is solely ours.

Making Sense

When putting together a room, be aware of how to engage every sense. Such attention to detail will take a space from solely functional to a place of retreat. Some ideas:

1 TOUCH: For a tactile experience, enlist fine china, silver, and crystal. Throw a soft blanket on a chair or a sofa to add warmth.

2 SIGHT: Choose your room's primary tone and then add an accent color for punch. Place special touches throughout, such as books, art, and natural elements like flowers and beach souvenirs. Consider how lighting can create impact in a room.

3 TASTE: Always keep edibles on hand that are easy to prepare, such as chocolates or mini appetizers, to entertain the impromptu guest.

4 SMELL: Add drops of rose essential oil to a burning candle or even burn your favorite essential oil in a pan of water to scent the entire home.

5 SOUND: Be in tune to always playing music. Keep trusted CDs on hand, turn on satellite radio, or log onto a playlist from your computer.

All of these pieces are unified by theme, color, and texture. The two chairs both have a weathered white patina similar to the architectural objects above. A generous use of pillows arranged in the corner of the bench seat beckons visitors to stay. [above left] This may be the perfect chair, with its deliciously stuffed cushion and a curve that cups you like a giant's hand. It receives sufficient support from cottagey accoutrements such as a wicker side table and pillows in enjoyable prints. [above right]

de-clutter

There is nothing less relaxing than a disorganized space, a room's version of the junk drawer. "It is always relaxing to enter a serene space," says Lizabeth McGraw of Tumbleweed & Dandelion. "Only decorate with what you need. I do a lot of editing. I love my things but only need a few pieces in my home, so each one has to be very special to stay."

Reassess scraps of paper that were important two tax seasons ago and the dried flowers from your cousin's wedding that you don't have the heart to toss. If you have a passion to collect, tame your keepsakes so they won't take over. We all have belongings that we want, but you must assess what you need. This approach gives you permission to remove the clutter, helping you design not just a well-thought-out space, but also one that's more accommodating to your desires. "My space needs to be comfortable and tidy. Everything has its place so the space is free of clutter, which allows me to think clearly. I've made it my own with fresh flowers, a fragrant candle, lots of books, and my wheaten puppy, Donovan, who is always close by," says Yvette Dobbie, a philanthropist who divides her time between California and Arizona.

Your room can be balanced and include your personal keepsakes while staying clutter free. Such harmony will work to the advantage of an attractive display. "I believe that a room should be filled with the things you love, but you also need to leave empty spaces," says designer Brooke Giannetti. "These clean spaces give your cherished objects room to breathe."

> " [There] seems to be within all of us an innate yearning to be lifted momentarily out of our own lives into the realm of charm and make-believe. "
>
> —DOROTHY DRAPER

The slogan "Keep Calm and Carry On" may have originated on posters in Britain during World War II to raise morale under the threat of attack, but it is well suited to the modern day for its design appeal. This room exudes tranquillity through all its simple details, while the vivid blue of the painting is the statement that brings interest to the setting. Seating choices abound, though thoughtful positioning of furniture does not infringe on space.

Making Room

To keep your room distinctive, stay true to the following tenets:

1 PERSONALIZE: Include accent pieces that have a story, such as mementos collected from a trip, gifts you've received, or arts and crafts created by human hands.

2 INVEST: Spend on items that will provide enjoyment and get wide use such as fine linens, art, and a one-of-a-kind piece of furniture.

3 SHOP AROUND: Hunt for special pieces at flea markets or online. Says Kathleen Delgado of Vintageweave Interiors, "Because I'm an antiques dealer, my most special pieces are quite old. Knowing that some family no longer on this earth once loved and cared for a piece makes my heart sing. It brought them joy and now brings me joy, which gives each special piece a soul."

4 EDIT: If something in your room seems out of place, eliminate it. Keep only those things that maintain a harmonious balance.

5 PRIORITIZE COMFORT: A room must always have one chair or sofa so comfortable it rivals the bed. However, comfort should not have to compete with style, as a great piece can look and feel beautiful with the right fabrics and accessories.

6 ENLIST THE FIVE SENSES: Run through a mental checklist to see if your room addresses every sense.

Signs of distress give a room a level of comfort and beauty that an overly designed room lacks. This nook includes all romantic flourishes: textiles, flowers, lighting, a mirror, and fabulous furnishings with a soothing patina. The soft tones of blue, with splashes of red, appeal to cottage lovers. [opposite]

come to your senses

When I was younger and began to take an interest in style, I looked to my mother for inspiration. She took risks that other mothers did not. She wore fitted vests with ties, she wore fedora hats, and she had a few fabulous coats for each season. She also came with a signature scent, Shalimar, which will forever be the scent of my mother. As a young teenager, I devoted my babysitting earnings exclusively to developing my style. I had smelled Ysatis on a friend and fell in love with the fragrance. This was the first and only time I granted the spritzer lady access to my bare wrist at a beauty counter.

After moving to college I learned that such attention to scent could also be applied to a room. The dorms worthy of an afternoon of procrastinating all had a scent, smells that did not result from the burning of incense or microwave popcorn. Some of my dorm mates used fragrant candles, while others had scented drawer liners and room spray. My room smelled of Southampton Rose, a Crabtree & Evelyn line that has sadly ceased production. Unlike my perfume, my preference in home scents has changed. Gardenia, lily, and orange jasmine comfort me more than does the aroma of chocolate chip cookies baking in the oven. It's this unseen detail of my room that captures a heightened sense of style.

family home

While practicality becomes the mode for living when children and their schedules rule the household, it's possible to step away from the conventional mom duties and teach family members the importance of good living. Michelle Tingler, founder of the blog Opinionated MAMA, which engages America's moms by discussing news and events from a mom's perspective, has a home that does not resemble the typical household of three kids, a dog, and a tortoise. It is highly stylish and efficiently arranged. "Live a little," she jokes. "We have a zillion kids running in and

Spectacular furnishings precisely arranged, and tones from nature such as wheat and moss, set a crisp foundation and the perfect forum in which to weave in items that Susan Feldman, founder of One Kings Lane, holds in high regard. The corner bookshelf contains books from her father's art studio. In fact, he created much of the artwork that fills the room. "If you fill a space with the things you love, no matter how eclectic, the space will speak to your personality," says Susan.

out all the time, and I wouldn't want it any other way. We love the things in our house and our things know it!"

Michelle is not afraid to use her finer items, even with the liability of active kids and pets. The things you love are meant to be used and enjoyed and should not be exclusive to the adult members of the house, "because every day is a special family occasion," says Michelle. "My kids eat off of china or paper plates; it just depends on what works. If you have some time, bust out the china. It's fun. Who cares? My wood pieces have rings on them, and slipcovers and zippers are my friends."

The British West Indies style is reflected in the accessories with an impressive array that offers visual punch. The pieces run the gamut from such exotic accessories as African beads, indigo textiles, and blue-and-white ginger jars. Finding such unique pieces is part of the fun for designer Susie Mitchell, who begins with a mental list of items she hopes to acquire before she hits flea markets. "That's where I can find funky older treasures, even art!"

a little lived in

When I style a home for a magazine shoot, my goal is to reflect the true essence of the resident. To rearrange a home so that the owner's finger-prints cannot be found right down to removing the smudges on a toaster does not reflect the personality of the dweller. I treat a home like a novel, where personal things, such as the arrangement of plates for an afternoon snack or a stack of letters waiting to be opened, are the everyday items that reveal the loves of the homeowner at her most uncomplicated.

A home that is too perfect is as itchy as a Shetland wool sweater. Such showcase rooms with matching wallpaper and fabrics and perfectly creased sheets are typically created with the help of a designer. Even the accessories on a table look more like showpieces than functional items or personal treasures. It is hard to feel at home in someone else's vision. Living with your own style is the cure-all for any design dilemma.

Gustavian Inspiration

Gustavian furnishings are light and delicate. They are undoubtedly elegant but are also quite practical when creating a functional room to retreat in. According to Ann Millang, the designer behind St. Barths Home and Swedish Blonde, such furnishings allow for the use of maximum space rather than becoming obstructions. "In the 1700s, especially in the manor homes, it was common to move the furniture to the edge of the room during parties so guests could dance all night long. As the party progressed ottomans and chairs could be moved around to fit a new activity."

Such an arrangement has its benefits in today's lifestyle. The possibility of moving items to accommodate certain needs adds to their functionality. You can decorate with items that speak to you but can be easily moved if you have a guest over.

"Most designs can have an elegance as well as a purpose. If you have a small bench, it usually has a hidden storage space under the seat," continues Ann. Her Drottningholm sofa is inspired by the elegant designs of the 1700s. Simply removing the back pillows allows it to be used as a sleeper. "I like that about Swedish design. There is beauty and always function," says Ann.

Red-and-white chairs huddled like an old married couple beckon leisurely activities. They are undoubtedly comfortable, while the vivid design keeps them from being frumpy. The bookshelves meet organizational needs with personal mementos set throughout. Painting the back paneling in matching red is a design technique that keeps the space original. [opposite]

making comfortable choices

Consider two chairs. One is wooden with spindly legs and a wicker seat. The other has more stuffing than a holiday bird, with a harem of cushions that seduces. I bet you'll choose the comfortable chair to sit in.

Though vanity has its place in a beautiful room, you won't be spending much time in it unless it's comfortable. Keep in mind where you will be doing most of your lounging, and make that chair, couch, or loveseat the focal point of the space. Then romanticize it with lighting and accessories.

Susan Ellison of Blue Springs Home begins the design process around comfortable sofas and chairs, which she arranges to make the most of the space. Furniture should never overpower a room; test out different placements for a few days each. "After the grouping has been arranged comes the fun part," says Susan. "Decide on color schemes and have fun with pillows, throws, and rugs to tie the grouping together. These can be changed seasonally."

Consider your space and what you aspire to achieve there: Will it be used for work, leisure, solitude, entertaining—or all of the above? Define your needs and decide what furnishings are required to meet them. In other words, choose a focal point upon which to base the furniture plan. Placement of furniture needs to be functional, so be selective about what pieces you bring in—excess is so passé. Acquire only pieces that provide both beauty and function to simplify your decorating mission. Susan Ellison likes to use fewer and larger pieces of furniture, no matter how small the room. Lots of little items will clutter a space.

turn on some light

Lighting can have a dramatic impact on a room's appearance. It elevates a mood in the same subtle way a good scent or music will. Lamps and chandeliers give off a more tranquil glow than the harsh glare of fluorescent light. Or simply burn candles to create a quiet mood.

Ambience can also be achieved through color and design choices. For instance, the Gustavian look masterfully builds on a room's light; with such long winters, the Swedes are gifted in finding brightness in a space. After visiting the Court of Versailles, the future king Gustav was inspired by the neoclassical style. This design evolved into the Swedish version with light colors and less ornate styles.

Designer Ann Millang lives in Sweden and thereby follows the tenets customary of this style. Her interiors are free of clutter and have a generous use of blonde wood as well as a pale color palette of pearl grays, ivory, and many shades of blue. Says Ann, "Here nature dictates a color palette of blues of the sea (as we are surrounded by so much water), straw colors from the fields, oyster white from the shells, and grays from natural rock outcroppings." Natural light from windows is also revered, and so curtains are often sheer and pale.

A space is contained within old shutter boards that frame an unusual columned mirror. The many shades of white keep the look from being too banal. Trusted go-to pieces—sterling silver serving ware, a tufted bench pillow, and an expansive table—invite leisurely activities.

read the room Many notes come together to create a harmonious look: A commonality in color, style, and personality creates a flawless execution. The dark floors and table contrast with light furnishings and collectibles from the sea, while blue-and-white ginger jars stay true to the British Colonial look. "Be sure to throw in an element of surprise," says Susie. The zebra-print ottoman adds a powerful statement. [opposite]

treasure chests A faux-bamboo hall tree in a neglected corner offers height and a place to showcase interesting textures and colors that tie into the room's theme. [above left] All the collections are thoughtfully arranged. "When accessorizing, group similar objects together so they will look more important," advises Susie Mitchell. [above right] Maritime art provides a stunning backdrop for the shell boxes, and old books add height and scale. [left]

Make It About Her
Add some life to a larger room with things that give off heat—a fire, candles, soft rugs, and throws.

tip the scales What could be a simple wall becomes a room's focal point when it's primped with artwork. Notice the three paintings in descending sizes atop shelves with carefully arranged books. The pairing is clean, far from cluttered, while gold and deep reds are used as the connecting colors. [above]

three in one Carve out three spaces within one room by thoughtfully arranging furniture. This room is cleverly divided into three segments by furniture arrangements that act as barriers. This visual trick creates a multipurpose room within one space. The room still maintains its coziness with a surplus of wonderful detailing. Classic toile, a tiled fireplace, and smartly assembled collections here and there are interesting elements that display nostalgia and personality. [opposite]

so vain The focal point in this setting is the unique vanity table, which was one of the first antiques Brooke Giannetti's husband bought after they were married. Such a keepsake makes this room truly personal and feminine. Brooke speaks of the piece as if it were an old friend, saying how she and her husband were struck by its unusual shape and painted finish. "Combined with Steve's drawings, my vanity adds to the romantic feel of our bedroom." The soft colors of red and blue sketches, framed elegantly in silver painted wood, provide a soothing tone. A jeweled picture frame, books, and perfume bottles set on the vanity pick up the color from the artwork, and their delicate scale keeps them from overpowering the table. [opposite]

one strong piece Your retreat must have a comfortable place to sit. The chair's plumpness and boxy style that could fit two make it romantic. The soft texture and floral pattern create the perfect setting for an afternoon tryst. [above left]

mutual interests When you decorate around your prized collectibles, you will achieve your most personal form of expression. Pieces that you choose will inevitably work together, as their "DNA" derives from your passions: What you find pretty typically shares a common color, period, or style. Lynn Goldfinger of Paris Hotel Boutique is a lover of silver and French antiques. Collecting has always been her passion. "I try to keep my collections down to a minimum: hotel silver, portrait paintings, and some vintage San Francisco memorabilia," she says. [above right]

Immortal Trends

Enduring designs include quality pieces made with precious metals or derived from nature. Classics are dependable additions to a woman's lair.

- Anything Art Deco will take you into a more luxurious time. This clock juxtaposed against a Chrysler Building figurine shines.

- An unusual shell-turned-candleholder holds court in this vignette.

- Animal prints will always rule a matriarchal kingdom.

From its clean lines, metallic shades, and glitzy origin, Art Deco is a design treatment that continues to appeal to followers of glamour. Beginning in the 1920s in Paris, its origins are illustrious. Iconic examples include the Chrysler Building in Manhattan, art by Tamara de Lempicka, and sculptures that look like hood ornaments on a luxury car. In this loft in Los Angeles's historic downtown neighborhood, the owner transforms the raw space with Art Deco flourishes. The walls are painted industrial gray. The furnishings are predominantly black, and silver piping that runs along the ceilings adds a bit of glint. Substantive bureaus provide space for such ornamental accents as bar accessories, quirky lamps, and candlestick holders. [opposite]

The New Eighteenth-Century Style

Rediscovering a French Décor

Text by MICHÈLE LALANDE
Photographs by GILLES TRILLARD

keep it clean Emphasize the importance of your quality things by setting them center stage as in a museum. An important piece of art is aptly highlighted with walls painted in a corresponding tone. Yes, you can base a wall color on the art! Objets d'art provide the perfect accent on a clean surface. The silver pheasants are especially important because they belonged to Susan Ellison's grandmother. "They remind me of her and they are one of those accessories that you can use a million different ways in different places," she says. With its simply arranged conversation pieces, this room achieves understated glam with the right touch of nostalgia. [opposite]

nature and art A luxurious coffee-table book is topped by a starfish, combining high art with the natural. [above]

Make It About Her
The same principle of adding more layers of clothing to keep you warm applies to home design. More accessories on the table, like an embroidered table runner, will create a cozier effect.

aging beautifully
Important pieces look better with time as they develop a soft patina and a one-of-a-kind aura. The mirror is painted in the most soothing shade of blue. The trim and bowed top connect all the pieces found on the credenza. Light walls and floors keep the look airy for a vignette that aims to soothe. [above left]

let it loose
A relaxed elegance is achieved through a balance of important pieces and a variety of seating that white chairs and couches provide. Slouchy pillows beckon relaxation both on the couch and in a corner nook. The mirror and chandelier work in tandem to call upon light. Small luxe details such as gilded papers tucked away and a silver tea set in an unusual shape engage the curious dweller. [above right and opposite]

modernist movement
Even a modern design can include classic elements. An angular couch (vaguely reminiscent of a fainting couch) and table are the focal points. Character pervades through the flowers and collectibles, and artwork depicting mountain climbers brings in a humorous touch. [following spread]

great shapes Neutral tones and lush throws create a calming effect, while quality accessories keep the room from looking like a boutique hotel lobby. From square pillows to silver orbs, shapes abound, creating a strong geometric sub-theme. Even the dining room chairs have a playful take from the cutout square backs. A fishbowl, a candle, and roses placed around the room reinforce the circular trend. On the coffee table, objects of interest are neatly arranged. With such neutral terrain, anything goes with an accent color. The addition of purple from the fishbowl and flowers strikes a regal tone.

Make It About Her
Play up the feathered piece at left by adding like-minded accessories to the room, such as feathers in a vase for a different take on a flower arrangement. More colors that pick up the subtle tones of purple can be transferred into additional art and accessories.

contrast colors Blue and brown is a color combination that is difficult to tire of. It can take on many forms, such as in a metallic-glazed vase, and it always delivers elegantly. Whether you use the scheme in a vignette or in a piece of art or develop an entire room based on these colors, it will soothe and be more engaging than pink for a male visitor. [above left]

calm down Certain accessories will instantly calm the most stressed, especially candles and remnants of the sea, which Loretta Kilheffer of Full Bloom Cottage judiciously uses to achieve soothing results. A stand of candles from a church is an unusual piece that evokes tranquillity. "They use them for prayer and services. I love it!" says Loretta. [above right]

say peace Designer Janet Solomon knows how to pacify. Her approach to living is calm, quiet, and beautiful. "A woman's space should always be the most peaceful room in a home," she says. "The elements that come to mind are air and reflection. A haven to rest, rejuvenate, and let her mind play." This vignette is inspired by a dove's nest, as noted from the feather-colored wall, a delicate birdcage, and decorative eggs. A column and a lamp stretch out the display, and the scalloped art piece links them together. "Burning a Cire Trudon candle scented with citrus, mint, and tea leaf is always a clean and fresh way for new inspiration to move in." Her choice in fragrance recalls a church, which correlates to the ecclesiastical art wonderfully highlighted beneath a dome jar. [opposite]

white and bright Dilemma: You want to design a single space with a variety of beautiful things. Solution: Keep the palette clean with a generous use of white and pieces that reflect your interests. This room is romantic with a modern take on neoclassical design. Touches of accent colors include gold trim and a subtle use of peach in the flowers and the throw. Mirrored and glass accessories are also used judiciously, notably with two chandeliers and mirrors. Long walls enlarge the space, while an oversized painting of roses becomes the statement piece that summarizes the room's romantic theme.

Make It About Her
Feminine touches can easily be brought in with gauzy draperies in lieu of woven wood, a delicate lamp, and a change of pillows.

designer digs Sally Bartz's colorful designs are found throughout the house in the form of art, upholstered chairs, and her bags from her own product line. One vignette focuses on an important piece of artwork that directs the palette. A colorful sampler is always a classic piece, especially alongside a modern desk clock in zesty yellow and family photos to personalize. Sally is the creator of Halsea, a line of women's accessories in classic retro sea-inspired prints endemic to "old school" California. She is skilled at creating the best from the past in a modern setting. The bag and tin are Halsea items, showing how her home and design aesthetic collide. "It's only natural that my favorite color combos appear in Halsea prints," says Sally. "Since I'm limited in the amount of Halsea items I can produce, my creativity spills over into little nooks and crannies in our house. Thankfully my husband is fairly tolerant of this!" **[left and above center]**

past presence You might find, as Sally has, that your most treasured spot in the home is actually a quiet nook in which to spend quality time with your child. As seen in her daughter's room, Sally's favorite room for its nostalgic appeal, retro prints and colors play well together. "It has a great, classic little-girl's-room feel with its fresh red-flowered wallpaper. A pale green velvet chair is the perfect spot for us to read books," says Sally. The highboy dresser loses its fussy formality with a coat of green paint. **[above right and opposite]**

orange pop Within an orange showcase, special items are amped to transform this space into designer Natalie Umbert's. A festive jug and salt and pepper shakers are silly and sweet. The table is modern, functional, and the accompanying Lucite chairs confirm its highly stylized design. A simple black shelf showcasing a retro fashion illustration and photograph of Natalie with her daughter is the most engaging detail. [above]

a colorful statement Color guides the look, with citrus tones that would rival an orange grove and blue and green for pop. Sally Bartz's prints are in their natural environment, and shine spectacularly. "It's just a home in which the décor happens to be guided by the same hand, heart, and eye that guides the Halsea line," Sally says. A shag zebra skin rug is a humorous take on the natural hide, showing a relaxed version of the iconic print. [opposite]

a timeless look A nook created by a stairwell becomes the most envied space
in the house. All the superb pieces share the same patina, and subtle touches of pink
are incorporated through the candles, the sconce, and the shading in the elaborate
clock, the most impactful statement in the grouping. "I chose to hang this large clock in
the hallway because of its unexpected scale and its warm colors," says designer
Brooke Giannetti. Without fail, visitors always comment on its originality. [opposite]

stay awhile Casually laid-out shoes speak volumes: long day. Tidying loses out
to needed rest. You have a guest over and though the shoes are pretty, you slip them
off to get comfortable. When they are patent pink heels that could double as a
weapon, they add a punch of color and interest to the design scheme. [above]

palatial surroundings Janet Rodriguez, owner of The Embroidery Palace, has a room in her home that reminds one of a royal seaside destination, with its nautical blue and red tones. The curtains in the doorway provide instant drama when one enters the space. The rug, pillows, window treatments, and chair upholstery all connect the same pattern and floral theme. Special pieces, such as a footstool and roundabout chair, are regal members of the setting. Shells transformed into art pieces are displayed here and there. The walls, painted blue with a suede-like finish, lend a cocooning effect to the room.

screen saver This Beverly Hills room pays homage to the designs of William "Billy" Haines, whose influence reigned during the period of Hollywood glamour with such clients as Nancy Reagan, Joan Crawford, and Marion Davies. A compilation of chairs upholstered in a variety of lush fabrics huddles up to tables, creating a balanced grouping of seating areas for easy entertaining. The layout also cleverly mimics the designs on the patterns. Asian and contemporary accents are monochromatic to fit the scheme and are highly styled. Flowers bring in a homey scent and feel.

the admiral's club A couch you'd expect to find in an airline frequent-flyer lounge sets the retro tone with its low back and clean lines. Pillows in unusual shapes and a romantic chinoiserie fabric pick up the Asian theme from the painting. [above]

signs of weather Metallic accessories and furnishings that show their patina are light, comforting, and classic touches that simulate nature's prettiest moments. An elegant couch with distressed trim correlates to the unfinished look in the mercury-glass containers. The simply framed prints of eggs are a tranquil and delicate addition. A grouping of pillows contributes color and comfort. [opposite]

Accommodating Guests

Too much me time can make even the most narcissistic women feel a bit cramped. Yes, you can get tired of your own company. There is also something sad about creating a fantastic space and having no one to share it with. When you let people into your favorite nook, you give them a window into yourself.

Elevate your go-to place by hosting company. Entertaining guests need not be a challenging affair. Simplify preparations and give your attention to details that take little effort. "Make guests feel at home," says Michelle Tingler. "I wanted to create a space where my friends and family could come in, plop down, and get cozy." Michelle's kitchen is perpetually stocked with bottled beverages and snacks so impromptu needs can be addressed. "More time to relax and enjoy each other's company!" she says.

When entertaining friends, never underestimate the power of a fabulous apron to capture the mood—precisely the kind of style worn to create a knockout Long Island iced tea along with 1950s cocktail fare. Prepare easy dishes that have classic appeal to pull guests into a more festive, nostalgic time.

Take some of the most classic entertaining ideas from the past and update them for a modern context. The overall style could look quite spectacular with little effort. Foods from earlier eras are comforting and festive, but they also must appeal to today's refined palates. Use fresh ingredients and employ your favorite bakery for a gorgeous dessert. A new look for the lobster rolls is a nod to small bites from the past. Beef purses with cream cheese wrapped in arugula are deceptively simple to create with a big wow factor.

time-shares

When sharing your space, there are certain considerations that demonstrate your hosting savvy. Flowers, drinks, and edibles make a guest feel at home. The more thoughtful the presentation, the more heightened the experience. Such a display need not look like the lobby of the Plaza Hotel. A simple cake can be garnished with garden clippings. Swap out floral arrangements from standard glass containers to your favorite vessel, such as a vase made from mercury glass and iron.

Kathleen Delgado of Vintageweave Interiors mixes her treasures by focusing on texture and height. Kathleen's principles also apply to entertaining. "I take an extra-large silver tray and mix in clear Depression and antique glass cordial glasses in varying heights and textures, such as ribbed glass, diamond glass, floral cut glass, and patterned glass," she says.

For Marisa Crawford, a Brooklyn-based photographer, hints from her past make their way into everything she presents. Cocktail hour is completely modern, yet the gathering is rooted in a richer, more textured

Ice cream sandwiches made of macarons in Easter-egg colors are an elegant twist on a favorite dessert. Continuing with the pastel foundation, match vintage pieces in calming patterns to make the arrangement your own. [above left] Elevate an ordinary spread into a lavish display by adding beauty to the everyday. A vessel found at a French flea market dramatizes a floral arrangement; figs become sinful when dipped in white and dark chocolate. Surround a simple rum cake with lavender clippings and you take a simple dessert to new heights. [above right]

period from her use of vintage items in modern settings. Every image tells a story. The same holds true for the way she dresses, decorates, entertains, and lives. "I am very much inspired by my mother's aesthetics," says Marisa. "She was raised in New York and graduated from art school in the 1950s, and she had the ladylike posture and style of the era."

Her home's style is inspired by her childhood memories; layers of classic fabrics and paper compose a tasteful home that is both lived-in and distinctive. "Our home was decorated with classic antiques upholstered in colorful Scandinavian prints. I will never forget a summer I went away when my mother had the house re-wallpapered and painted, which led to my obsession with the best wallpaper." Her passion shows in the way she entertains. With a nod to her childhood, she uses an abundance of vintage pieces she grew up with, and she serves the delectable dishes her mother once made. Creating a home based on childhood memories provides the comforting feelings you never want to lose hold of. To share this with others is the quality of a great hostess.

good stock

The prototype of an efficient room, which provides enough comforts to rival your entire home, is a hotel suite—a nice one that gets ink in the tabloids because of a celebrity tryst. The foundation of an inviting hotel room is a comfortable couch, a flat-screen TV, and a bed so neatly tucked you could do mat exercises on it. Upon arrival you may eschew all of the amenities and head straight for the mini fridge that so tempts you to pay the 100-percent markup for a bag of salted almonds. Your favorite room can accommodate people in the same way without the antiseptic aftertaste.

Nourish company with food and drink. Always have snacks on hand, whether in the pantry, in the refrigerator, or in a mini fridge installed in a handy place. Easy-to-prepare appetizers such as dips and sliced artisan bread satisfy and look great with very little arranging on a serving dish. Dress up cheeses with drizzled olive oil or fruit glazes. Serving a dish as simple as deviled eggs, presented well, can create the festive atmosphere one might expect from a holiday party. Channel a more classic era and whip up the foods and cocktails in the manner of a skilled hostess.

"A man's home is his wife's castle."

—ALEXANDER CHASE

use the good stuff

From a casual visitor to attendees at an invitation-only event, guests should be treated to the same presentation no matter what the celebration. So share your finer serving items and china with guests. Pull out the dainty plates, crystal, and serving trays from hard-to-reach places so they can be called upon regularly.

Says Marisa Crawford, "Just the same as 'the shoes make the outfit,' my rule for entertaining is to have a foundation of great china and fine linens, silver, and crystal. You could just serve water and toast and it will be the best toast and the best water your guests ever had."

Such a functional piece could have been anything—shelves, a changing table—but it works perfectly as a bar area thanks to its convenience and natural coloring. Slim rattan baskets organize drinks and accessories, and larger items are given room on the bottom shelf. [opposite] Formal glasses do not have to be limited to toasting holiday celebrations; gussy up a simple smoothie with your favorite pieces. [above]

Stock the Bar

ALCOHOL: Have all the essential spirits, which include vodka, gin, rum (dark and light), whiskey, and tequila, along with red and white wine. Purchase affordable brands, which you will be more inclined to use over pricier options.

MIXERS: The basics to keep on hand are tonic water, club soda, cola, and ginger ale. The main juices are orange, cranberry, grapefruit, and tomato. Lime juice, grenadine, and simple syrup are used for the kind of cocktails enjoyed on the 5:29 p.m. bar car headed to New Canaan, Connecticut. Stock up on premade mixers for margaritas, daiquiris, and piña coladas. And don't forget a bag of ice in the freezer. Having the essential mixers on hand shows guests that you're prepared to meet their needs.

BAR ACCESSORIES: The staples include a bottle opener, a corkscrew, a cocktail shaker with strainer, napkins, straws, a measuring glass, an ice bucket, a blender, coasters, stirrers, and umbrellas.

GARNISHES: These should include olives, cherries, lemons, and limes; salt and sugar for rimming the glasses.

GLASSWARE: Keep to the basics to save on space but still have room for multiples. Have on hand four to six cocktail, old-fashioned, hurricane, and red and white wine glasses and a few martini and shot glasses.

the bar is open

Furnish your entertaining area with a simple bar. A trolley, a small credenza, or a cart is a stylish way to showcase bar accessories in the most space-challenged rooms. It also pays homage to a more glamorous time while encouraging the fun and sophisticated ritual of the cocktail hour. From Art Deco to distressed wood, any cart will do; just search for one with layered shelves and a clean look.

According to Lynn Goldfinger of Paris Hotel Boutique, her silver trolley originated as a carving station that an upscale hotel or dining establishment would use. "It would have been a focal point for any fine French restaurant. Once rolled tableside by a white-jacketed restaurant captain for a showy carving of prime rib, this Art Deco carving station has now been reborn," says Lynn.

"What would you like to drink?" Such a question rolls off the tongue in the vixen-like manner of a Hitchcock heroine, but should not be posed unless you have a stocked bar. A small bar should include the main spirits, mixers, bar accessories, and glasses.

make a statement

You can enjoy entertaining guests when you choose a more intimate space and decorate it to the nines but on a smaller scale than it takes to decorate a larger room. You can change styles to suit the occasion, as the setup can easily be dismantled after the fun is over. Go bold—Alice-in-Wonderland's-tea-party bold. Such a setting is certain to cause smiles.

Noel Solomon is the artist behind the French-inspired paper art of Fanciful Designs. Noel has built a career around fabricating the kind of large paper flowers that would make Alice feel at home. Flamboyance meets romance in her vision. Her "fleurs," as she refers to them, are made from high-quality French paper. Their neutral white color can add flair to any surrounding.

Artist Noel Solomon's personal statement comes in the form of paper flowers she creates by hand. The flowers are the truest form of artistic expression in the room and, in a sense, create a theme-park effect for adults. [above and previous page]

For the setting of her entertaining area, Noel chose an ultra-feminine foundation that creates a Crystal Palace effect. Staple pieces like French slipcovered chairs, chandeliers, and linen pillows are versatile and practical but keep the look uncluttered. A palette of Icelandic blue, silver, white, gray, and hints of blush pink entrance like a production of *Swan Lake*.

Noel takes inspiration from her art of flowers and beautiful papers with functional lasting appeal. The paper flowers can be displayed as wall art or used as napkin rings or as a centerpiece that won't expire after a week. Such practicality adds to their appeal, and is the main reason why Noel adores working with them. "If I don't fall in love with my pieces I would never expect anyone else to," says Noel. "The paper fleurs are so versatile. I have had them framed, or I'll simply find any old vintage frame and arrange the fleurs in a cascading fashion within."

Noel creates her paper flowers on a large scale. The flowers can also be delicate, as used on the paper fleur napkin rings for an elegant table setting. "Their function is endless, and they're so fabulous as each one is torn by hand from high-quality French paper. Just as in nature, there are no two alike, which is another reason why I love them," says Noel.

Read the Classics

Know how to make classic cocktails by memory or keep a drink recipe book on hand. Here are recipes for iconic drinks:

martini

FOR: James Bond, cocktail hour, and ladies who can outwit their man [opposite, above]

2½ ounces gin or vodka
½ ounce dry vermouth
Orange slice, for garnish (optional)
Olives, for garnish

Pour the gin or vodka and the vermouth into a mixing glass filled with ice cubes. Stir for 30 seconds. Strain into a chilled cocktail glass. Add the orange, if desired. Garnish with olives.

manhattan

FOR: Sunset at the club, rainy afternoons with park views [opposite, below left]

2 ounces whiskey
1 ounce sweet vermouth
1 dash bitters
2 to 3 cherries
1 twist of orange peel

Combine the whiskey, vermouth, bitters, and ice cubes in a cocktail shaker. Shake well, until chilled. Strain the drink into a martini glass. Garnish with cherries and the orange twist.

brandy alexander

FOR: Fireside at the lodge, chocolate lovers [opposite, below right]

1½ ounces brandy
1 ounce crème de cacao
1 ounce heavy cream
2 ice cubes

Mix all the ingredients in a cocktail shaker or blender. Strain into a chilled cocktail glass.

mix, shake, enjoy A gorgeous Art Deco credenza with Asian panels gives pause to visitors. Accessories in glass and silver contribute to the clean look. A chrome milkshake blender weaves in another glamorous era. This hostess clearly reveres cocktail hour. **[above]**

vintage hotel glamour Says Lynn Goldfinger of her entertaining area: "Having a stocked bar with accessories reminds me of an old Hollywood movie. Some sophisticated gent or gal would always pull out a fancy crystal decanter and pour a guest a cup of scotch. It's so glamorous looking in the movies, or imagining the bygone days, that I thought I'd re-create it using accessories like vintage crystal decanters, sterling liquor tags, and glass swizzle sticks. Although we rarely use the bar for entertaining, it still adds a touch of glamour to the décor." Her serving trolley comes with its original bucket holder, au jus plate, and silver-plated kerosene burner to effectively pull visitors into another era. **[opposite]**

mask appeal Elevate your serving pieces with throwbacks to a saucier time. A cat mask will bring out the vixen in the most reserved hostess. **[opposite]**

going up A vintage bellboy hat in a signature color inspires the theme of a gathering: lobby bars, cocktail dresses, and "another round, please." **[above left]**

stick with a classic Funny napkins and swizzle sticks are always festive. An assortment of swizzle sticks in a glass container holds its own as a statement piece. **[above right]**

eye candy An open presentation of edibles and beverages makes guests feel welcome to help themselves without imposing on their host. Incorporate attractive display containers and play with color. **[left]**

food coloring Dress up everything you serve, treating edibles the way you would a room. The figs, cake, flowers, and plate all share the tones of purple, deep blue, and crimson.

calling collect Lynn Goldfinger creates a perfect blend of practical items with one of her favored collectibles: hotel accessories that typically relate to her home of San Francisco. **[above left]**

green is good Perrier, another late-eighties symbol of decadence that said, "Yes, I am fabulous. I will pay extra for sparkling water because I can." Decades later and the bottles sit in a more humbled, fanciful context. The glass parlays beautifully aside a wonderful fluted pedestal bowl in the same hue. Apples show an attention to detail. **[above right]**

Home Work

Some of the most exciting personal achievements are realized during a working moment. You come up with an idea for a new product; or you find the inspiration to create the next big trend. Thus, you need your own area in which to operate. "Every woman needs a sanctuary—a place to tune out, relax, read, write letters, and recharge in today's hectic world," says philanthropist Yvette Dobbie. Whatever your creative calling, a functional work space is vital.

A million ideas can collide into your next great project when you are settled in a space that inspires.

An office need not be a shrine to staplers and computer gadgetry. Designer Laura Lambert gives a simple but styled treatment to the shell bottles that she made. **[above]** The black and white imagery pairs nicely with a desk lamp that looks like a miniature studio light and a throw shows an attention to texture and comfort. **[opposite]** A line of vintage cameras on a shelf shares the black and white composition and echoes the "working" theme of the space. **[following spread]**

A woman caught in a creative moment is a woman at her best. Her mysteries and secrets are locked away in her mind, selectively siphoned to the world like limited-edition perfume. An arsenal of trusted essentials is sure to ignite the creative process: takeout from Empire Szechuan, magazine clippings, her son's pet rock, gorgeous paper, and colored pencils. She can't put a value on her computer, considering everything that is stored within it. Thus, a valued space to create is her office area.

Creating such a space cannot be achieved with just a trip to a standard office-supply store. Tape dispensers, thumbtacks, and rubber bands lack the soul found in markers artistically arranged like flowers or a screen

saver glowing with a vintage Chanel ad. A work area need not be elaborate. It should contain all the essentials that help you operate. For some, this could be a laptop or a French easel. Others may need tokens of inspiration—fabrics, art—and controlled lighting to help their mind reach a lucid level. Because a work area must inspire while being efficient, work necessities need to be organized, and mementos that motivate the mind should be easily visible and add beauty without encroaching.

> "A woman must have money and a room of her own if she is to write fiction."
>
> —VIRGINIA WOOLF

Laura finds another opportunity to make a statement in a passed-over spot. A fantastic bamboo-trimmed desk is the focal point. She loads up on shell art and flowers for a colorful arrangement that speaks to her designer's eye for all things relating to nature. [opposite] Chocolate is tempting as a visual in addition to being a good excuse to break from work. Use a patterned dish to fancy up the display. [above]

Show Some Tack

Assembling an Inspiration Board

Travel back to the days when you were assigned a school locker. With the twirl of three secret numbers you unlocked your personal sanctum. What was tacked inside that valuable real estate was less a fashion spread torn from a magazine than it was clues to your identity more telling than a blood sample. These clippings revealed your style, gave you inspiration to get through the daily grind, and lent background color to your personal place. The same holds true for an inspiration board in a work space, only on a more grown-up scale.

An ideal space for your board is above your computer. For those moments when you want to wander off your screen for a much-needed diversion, a look at what motivates you may be just the jolt to help you finish a task. Creating a board is simple. You can use a plain corkboard found at most office-supply stores; or take the look even farther by painting it your preferred color or covering it in wallpaper, wrapping paper, or fabric (easily attached with a staple gun). Crisscrossing ribbon is another popular treatment.

Slowly and deliberately your board will take form, filled in with the most colorful pieces that shape your mind. Include personal ephemera to add beauty, such as:

- invitations
- letters
- postcards
- ticket stubs
- photo-booth pictures
- ribbons

Over time, as you add and subtract elements, the board will become a constant stream of inspiration.

We all save little pieces of history for a reason, but the dilemma always arises as to where they should go. The ever-dependable inspiration board organizes such important pieces better than folders or a laptop. Says Yvette Dobbie, "I keep the board next to my desk, which has cherished and found objects, postcards from my travels, letters from dear friends, heart-shaped rocks from my walks at the beach, photos of my loved ones, fun things that make me happy. These feed my soul and are a constant reminder of what is important in my life—where I've been and where I'm going." [above]

golden era This office corner is positively Jane Austen–esque with its lush detailing. The look begins with a beautifully constructed desk that has legs as slim as a runway model's. The golden tone that sets the mood extends to the paneled wall, textiles, and desk accessories. **[opposite]**

rich in detail The desk accessories are all appointed with a theme of elegant lives once lived. The portraits, feathers, and other ephemera are organized on an inspiration board made from an old frame. Small frames within spotlight interesting portraits. Even the vintage desk set conjures up wonder about past owners. But flowers bring the look into a modern context and comfort comes through in small chair pillows that share a complementary print. **[above and left]**

Make It About Her
Warm up the coolness of concrete with a colorful rug. Candles provide immediate girly touches.

office shed It's a common story: Home and professional lives blur, and working on the kitchen table proves to be an unsatisfactory operation. The shed in the back of the house whose last residents were a pack of raccoons may be the answer to the office dilemma. Once the garden rakes and camping gear are cleared out, a space emerges. Here, a cherished wicker desk and chair fit perfectly by the window, which lets in painterly light. Finished with vintage finds, this space is design worthy of a movie set. **[above]**

open-and-shut case A rolltop desk is a classic combination of function and design. There is a writer's tone in this setting, from the rich burled-wood desktop, old books, and traditional accessories found in a Regency novel. The dainty blue-and-white teacup is a comforting detail that pulls in another set of colors. **[opposite]**

if the mood should arise While a great old barn in the woods is a romantic notion of an artist's studio, creating a place to paint within your office area is more realistic. Yvette Dobbie's painting area continues her theme of using fabulous pieces for everyday needs: Note the fine china used as a paint palette. A Hello Kitty surfboard is a great statement about her casual manner. **[opposite and above]**

DOGS MUST BE CARRIED

ppy mother's day

Rings from Braden Ro...
new jewelry collection, ...
Post 26 in Brentwood and ...
Hollywood's Roseark. ...
In the sitting room, a ...
...orite movie of Ro...
...es fou...

nesting

HOM...

S...

SOPHIE SCHULTE-HILLEN
beauty & lifestyle editor

Fashion | STUDIO STARS

<< WHY CALIFORNIA Born and rais... Venice, Keenan feels a deep connection to the area and her family, who still lives in the beachside enclave. OBSESSED WITH Metal in all its forms, from architecture to sculpture. "I especially love gold for its warmth, pliability and softness. DESIGN SIGNATURES Her line, Angus, is full of rough, organic textures. "Even I don't always know how a piece is going to turn out," she says. MUSES Her fiancé and family. "I draw from their adventurous spirit and grounded strength." GOOD LUCK CHARM "My hands, HAD ENOUGH OF "The disposability of everything." which both display my engagement ring and can work with metal." SECRETLY COVETS Beachfront property. PRICE RANGE $350 to $5,200. AVAILABLE AT Kaviar and Kind, L.A.

ANGELIQUE KEENAN

>> WHY CALIFORNIA "L.A. is totally creative in a nature-based kind of way," says the Kaviar and Kind co-owner. "I love watching bobcats sip water from the pool." OBSESSED WITH ...oth that lies within...

personal needs Homeowner Maria Tam carved out an office space in the far corner of her dining room. She sits next to a window through which she can watch her son skateboarding on a ramp that has taken over the backyard. "Despite having a small work space, I try to surround myself with things that I love and things that inspire me," says Maria. She foregoes the utensils for the convenience of takeout and refreshes her mind by revisiting significant mementos, like pictures of her son, cool cards from friends and loved ones, and magazine tear outs. **[opposite and above left]**

cottage industry Next to Maria's desk, dining room glasses perch on a shelf alongside useful books and papers. "Honestly," she confesses, "our cottage is so small that the area off the dining room and kitchen was the only place we could fit a work space for me. I do love it because it gets great afternoon light and because our kitchen and dining area are the heart of our home." Maria finds it practical to work in her home's nucleus, as it keeps her in the middle of her life's happenings. **[above right]**

Behind the Scenes

Lidy Baars is the woman behind the antiques shop French Garden House. A glimpse into where it all happens reveals part of the story about what makes her company so enchanting. She finds comfort in an ever-changing display of beautiful things and is known to reshuffle her interiors constantly for a change in inspiration. "I could display gilded antique French jewelry caskets alongside a collection of Victorian doll heads and antique French opera crowns. The next month, it could be vintage mannequins, antique baby dresses, and French Victorian photographs," says Lidy.

SPACE SOLUTIONS: Her office is small and efficient, with shelves, white storage boxes, and filing cabinets. "As an antiques dealer, I need lots of storage to hold all the smalls that I sell, and it needs to be so orderly that I can instantly pull one of the hundreds of those pieces from inventory when it sells," she says.

NEUTRAL PALETTE: Lidy chose a simple white, cream, and brown palette so it will blend in with an ever-changing roster of antiques. "While the bones of my office may be practical, it's those unusual decorations that make it a fun, inspiring place to be every day. I fill my office with things I love—quirky, beautiful, slightly shabby, or completely tattered things that catch my eye and make my heart beat faster," says Lidy.

special delivery

Every day at work—and she does work each day—Lidy Baars endeavors to transform the ordinary into the extraordinary. If she peddles an environment of aspiration, she must live by it. "Fresh flowers from the garden and beautiful music are a must for my working happiness," she says. **[above left and left]**

love notes

A bouquet of red pencils shows the beauty in the quotidian. Antique letters tied in a grosgrain ribbon elicit curiousity. Scrabble pieces spell out "Happily Ever After." These are the everyday elements that inspire Lidy in her work space. She becomes quite sentimental about the fairy-tale notion of her daily message, and immediately cites her husband and "best friend" as her muse. The letters are a beautiful touch and rekindle the art of letter writing and beautiful script words. She explains: "The little bundles of old letters are so heart-wrenchingly touching, a reminder of love, family, and friendship. No text message or e-mail will ever replicate that." **[above right]**

take note Right down to a pink notebook, every desk accessory should be considered when creating a thoughtfully designed office space. **[above]**

compilation piece If thoughts could be visualized, perhaps they would look something like an inspiration board. Pale pink walls almost become pop-rock cool juxtaposed with the quirky personal memorabilia. **[opposite]**

a playful mix
Yvette Dobbie is all work *and* play. She is a philanthropist and activist and looks like a 1960s film star even when she's cleaning out the garage. It's no wonder that her office area is a colorful mix of pretty things. Yvette has no qualms about using elegant pieces in unexpected ways, such as a mirrored tray and glass vase to contain markers. And nothing will ever get done without fresh flowers. **[above left and opposite]**

note to self
If you need a reminder of all those traits you aspire to, Post-it notes are most helpful. **[above right]**

loyal slippers
For days that are taking a crash dive, sliding tired feet into bunny slippers brings perspective. Life need not be taken too seriously. **[right]**

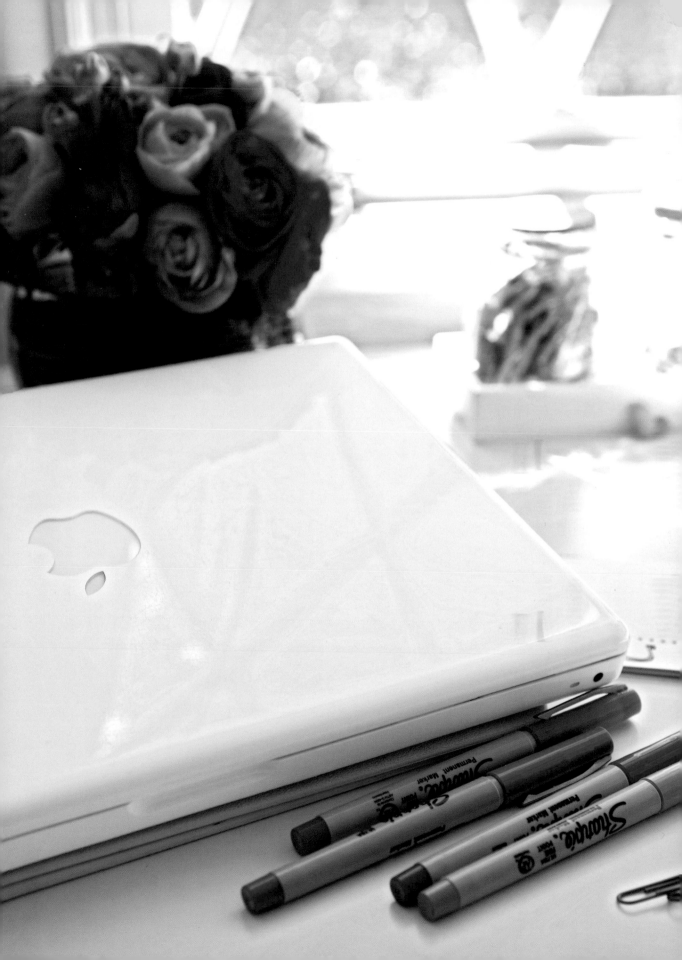

Take It Outside

The scent and feel of the outdoors tantalizes, and an entire day can be restructured just so you can spend it outside. Being outdoors calms, refreshes, and invigorates you. Thus, an outdoor space designed for your needs becomes vital for days that call for it.

This "room" may be missing walls and have a ceiling that never ends, but you can carve out a space with found objects and pieces more associated with the home to create an outdoor retreat filled with favorite accessories that will rival your most elaborate indoor room. Outfit it with basic needs to sustain a leisurely afternoon, such as reading material, pillows, a light blanket or throw, snacks, and beverages. Such a romantic principle to designing a space will relegate the indoors as a nice place to "visit" when inclement weather beckons.

Architectural paneling creates the illusion of an outdoor room. Columns and a distressed table add symmetry, while the addition of linens offers color and texture.

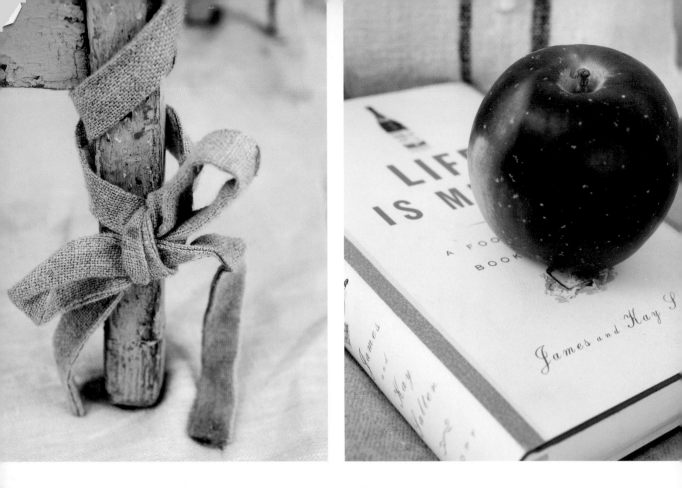

Even the smallest of details can make a major impact. A bench tied with a
burlap bow, heavy French textiles, and a favorite read are one-of-a-kind design
techniques for a truly personal space. [above] Search flea markets, estate sales, and
consignment shops for unusual finds to mark your outdoor space as your own
design. Look for jugs, baskets, bistro chairs, and a unique chaise longue to
complete the space. [opposite]

inside out

The same principles that apply to creating a retreat indoors come into
practice for the outdoors. Though your "ceiling" might change like a
hologram as clouds pass by, and your walls and accessories might be pro-
vided by trees, flower beds, and the occasional furry visitor, you still crave
the textural elements that comfort you—and perhaps you crave them even
more so when exposed to the elements. Susan Ellison, proprietess of Blue
Springs Home, agrees. "Bring the indoors outdoors!" she says. "My
favorite spot in my home is the little patio outside the living room." Just
open the doors and step into an extension of the living room. A bench

nestled next to rosebushes and lined with vintage linen pillows makes an inviting spot for morning coffee or quiet meditation. Surround the space with plants and trees that create an inviting ambience. "I prefer gravel to grass. It's easier, and the gravel gives a texture to your plants and flowers. When you are inside your home, you should be able to look out all windows and see beauty. The outside should be a reflection of your home," says Susan.

laying it out

Identify your plot and what elements you desire to make it comfortable. If it is too sunny during certain times of the day, provide shade with an umbrella or high shrubbery. A love of gardening is not essential when creating your outdoor retreat. Visit your local nursery and source plants that require minimum care and thrive in your space's climate and soil. Pots of plants can help you achieve the look of a garden without calling upon a shovel. For the garden enthusiasts, when you spend time fostering your plants, you'll feel more of a connection to your personal space because you've tended it.

a few easy pieces

Outdoor furniture such as benches, tables, and chairs, and garden accessories such as columns, a wheelbarrow, a hammock, or trellises, are the sculptural pieces that provide ornamentation. They take the look from humble outdoor space to something more inviting and livable. Further accessorize with baskets, pillows, blankets, and outdoor lamps.

A garden need not look like a formal composition of flowers from an English estate; simplify the look by weaving in greenery that complements the yard's natural form.

Make It About Her
Accessorize with color, such as pots of flowers, to make the space lusher. Select flowers for their color and scent. Hidden speakers pumping music throughout are a suitable accompaniment.

let nature take its course Beautifully appointed gardens bring out the kid in us; we never want to go back inside. Nature is the designer here, and you can just add details to her work of art such as benches, stepping-stones, and birdbaths. [above left]

stretching the limits No wall is too short when creating a memorable room. Few of us live in manor houses, but outside, your walls are endless. This outdoor space, though grand, is contained within the area of a stone "floor." Two chairs and whimsical ball-shaped pillows express exclusivity. [above right]

waterside attraction Privacy is afforded in this pool area by the landscaping and series of levels. A few lounge chairs are semi-hidden on the upper level, where shade and the sound of the pool's fountain will lull the chairs' occupants to sleep. [opposite]

sustainable living Susan Ellison has given her home an extension with multiple garden rooms, which she enjoys daily. She'll have breakfast at the table in front of her house or lose reading time to a nap on a chair. Her garden is sustainable—mostly herbs, which are easy to grow; she features them in her cooking and in decorating her kitchen. A generous helping of strong and colorful textiles is always on hand. Splashes of red pick up the lead color of her garden flowers.

so succulent Sustainable plants in heavy pots are an easy way to share natural beauty. [above left]

exotic locales It may be just a backyard nook, but that doesn't have to keep your mind from wandering off to faraway places. Take a cue from Barcelona, Marrakech, or Istanbul with punchy textiles. [above right and opposite]

entertaining simplified You can have guests over whenever you want without ever having to go indoors. Sangria is always a welcoming elixir and looks great with vibrant John Robshaw linens. [left]

vintage pieces Using finer pieces in an outdoor setting creates a relaxed elegance. Natural-toned cutlery and fine linens keep a soothing shade that works well against the chippy blue table. Shell-rimmed place mats relax the setting. [opposite and above]

on the hot seat Take classic Adirondack chairs to a more stylish dimension with an haute aqua color. Towels purchased from Shutters on the Beach hotel in Santa Monica, a surfboard, and flowers in a vibrant contrast of orange tantalize the senses. [right]

on seating arrangements "I created several seating areas in our backyard, so that we can have meals outside or relax while entertaining friends. Filled with roses and hydrangeas, the garden is the perfect extension of our home. Treating those outdoor rooms just like rooms inside, I layer on pillows and tablecloths from my collections to make it all comfortable as well as beautiful," Lidy Baars says. [opposite]

see how her garden grows There is not a vacant spot of soil in Lidy's backyard with all of the rosebushes, ferns, and pots of plants. Flowers travel along the trellis. Garden clippings fill vases and pitchers, always ready for a table setting. Lidy thoroughly takes in the Southern California lifestyle. At least half of her year is spent in the garden, carefully planning a selection of flowers for color as well as interest, so it's important that her garden also be a relaxing retreat in which to reflect. [above]

safari retreat Think Rudyard Kipling and create an outdoor vignette with tents, a chest, cots, rugs, binoculars, and anything tortoise-rimmed.

british colonial defined Take a cue from the British, who took more than their language and customs to exotic terrain in the age of colonialism: They also took along comforts of home and mixed them with exotic finds as they experimented with new ways to mix cultures and design.

Make It About Her
Pile on the texture with a cotton throw, a robe, and a pillow.

Really Put Together

While you don't want to fall victim to an overly maintained home, rooms in which each item has its place are inviting and comfortable. A well-thought-out arrangement will make it less likely for you or a guest to casually throw belongings about. An organized system is the key to keeping your space from falling into disarray.

Clever organization includes smart storage and innovative display and can be the best trick for personalizing a room. For homes that have limited space, an armoire, a display case, or shelving is especially useful. Tuck away the yoga pants and the Laura Ingalls nightgowns while giving your more important items the proper venue in which to show off their beauty.

The calming colors of ice blue, silvery gray, and white keep an organized space looking light and inviting.

Get clever when arranging bookshelves. Removing jackets or showing the fantastic gilded-paper sides are a couple tricks to employ. Pair with like-minded accessories to complete the look.

When displaying your special pieces, keep the vignette linked through a common color, theme, texture, and look. If you are the bookish type who must live with your college-edition philosophy book, control the chaos by setting up an attractive shelving unit, or consider built-ins.

containing one's self

Every morning when you open your closet, you consider wearing a construction helmet for fear of what might fall out. Linens are in a tangle, and the dishes are haphazardy arranged, inviting a calamity. And how did you accumulate all this stuff? Though buying paper towels in bulk seemed like a good idea at the time, dwellers in a space-challenged home should reconsider.

We accumulate a great deal. While letting things go can be therapeutic, it can also be as difficult as breaking up with someone who just doesn't share the same goals. Consider using unconventional containers—even some knockout pieces—for storage.

"I organize the necessities in a room with baskets or other interesting storage options. For instance, I have old baskets on the tables next to the bed with all the things I need before I go to sleep; eyeglasses, medicines, hand creams, reading material are all in an attractive basket. Out of sight, but conveniently hidden," says Susan Ellison of Blue Springs Home. Susan also enlists unexpected pieces for her storage needs, such as a special old metal crate just for the firewood. "It keeps the wood off the floor and adds special interest to the room. It looks like a piece of sculptural art," she adds.

public display of affection

Organization need not be a science. A room's comfort level is elevated when you are surrounded by delicate and beloved things. Therefore, showcase your belongings in an overt display of affection. Jewelry, perfume bottles, and hair accessories can be laid out on a vanity table. Attach a peg shelf to the wall for your necklaces; this will give your jewelry more attention and perhaps even more wear thanks to easy access. Teacups and books will forever be an elegant combo, and they appear all the more feminine when grouped with pieces that are unified in style.

Organized spaces are the foundation of a beautifully kept home. Employing simple techniques, and perhaps investing in some handsome storage pieces, will make your space more attractive and usable.

> **"A good home must be made, not bought."**
> —JOYCE MAYNARD

Shelves are more than just an effective way to stow away favorite books; they can become a conduit to your personal style by being paired with favorite keepsakes, such as china, photos, and art. For more impact, group them in a variety of levels.

she's smart, too To designate one area for the sole purpose of making yourself pretty is the perfect embrace of the practice of being girly. The dressing area of Carrie Davitch, proprietress of Maude Woods, is a shrine to her most beautiful things: jewelry, family photos, and her wardrobe. **[opposite]**

caught up A traditional accordion-style Peg-Board finds an unconventional use for hanging necklaces. Such a technique combines function and style by showcasing the prettiest belongings and keeping them within reach. Accessorizing outfits in the mornings is easier when you can see all of your options at once. **[above]**

think outside the box This daguerreotype of ancestor photo combines personal history and beauty to this shelf's vignette. Propped up against opera glasses is a great way to combine decorative accents with function. **[above]**

set apart Release your favorite jewelry pieces from containers for a dainty, original display. **[opposite and following pages]**

on the scent Only a woman can understand the importance of her personal fragrance. She might have one signature scent or a variety that is selected based on her mood of the day. Glass perfume bottles containing honey-colored liquid catch the light. An arrangement of perfumes is a staple in any woman's lair. **[opposite]**

dolled up Lipstick, powder puffs, and a scented candle signify a woman who knows how to primp. Such tokens of femininity create a beautiful vignette. **[above]**

open view Neatly arrange collections on shelves around a shared theme, such as glass in light pink colors, baskets filled with vegetables, or souvenirs from the sea. These are the interesting personality pieces that distinguish a woman's style.

showpieces An antique cabinet is distinctive for its papered back panel in a soft floral pattern. The print on the china complements the theme.

reading list Book lovers do not have to give up their excessive volumes to a thrift store, as books can be cleverly arranged. While shelves are a time-honored method for displaying books, take the look further with a piece that arranges books as if they were modern art. Position them near a voluptuously shaped chair to complete the setting and invite perusing.

book smarts Shelves of varying sizes and shapes can turn a mass of books into something eye-catching. Position collectibles seemingly at random, such as vintage family photos or something that speaks to a unique interest like mother-of-pearl opera glasses or a seaside souvenir.

herbal essence There is a constant quandary with small households of where to put necessities without everything looking like a flea market stall. Armoires are the go-to piece, while their doors entice us to open them. Treat the inside of an armoire the way you would open shelving by placing like-minded items in tranquil colors. This piece stands on a bureau for added space to showcase such earth bounties as a rosemary plant and French linens. **[opposite]**

beautiful inside and out It's no wonder that the armoire has been a piece depended on for centuries—it's completely versatile. Armoires outfitted with shelves are decorative and a storage saver. Gustavian colors of ice blues and gray create a calming effect that works beautifully with every season. **[above]**

treasure trove Glass doors on this attractive piece are an opportunity to wield personal decorative flair. Shell art and books carry out the surf, beach, and fashion themes. **[following page]**

Show-and-Tell

A roomy closet is as valuable a commodity as a Manhattan parking space. Armoires are the pretty stepcousins of the closet, as they enhance the look of a room while providing much-needed storage space. Here's how to make the most of them:

- Armoires are attractive furnishings and revealing what's inside can enhance their look. Look for armoires with glass panes, or remove the doors for more exposed viewing of the shelving.

- Naturally, what you place within an armoire must be pleasing to the eye; therefore your finest china, books that share the same color, and collectibles all add to the visual impact.

- Group similar objects in neat stacks. Place other pieces of interest here and there, such as a painting or an assemblage of colorful bottles, to weave in an accent color against the neutral foundation.

- Play with the color scheme by painting the inside of the armoire in a contrasting color. The original wood finish beneath a painted exterior is equally inviting; or wallpaper the back panel as another decorative option.

where to find everything

astier de villatte
astierdevillatte.com

atelier natalie umbert
ateliernatalieumbert.com

blue springs home
Costa Mesa, California
(949) 642-3632
bluespringshome.com

kerry cassill
Laguna Beach, California
(949) 497-4422
kerrycassill.com

18th century atelier
British Columbia, Canada
(604) 886-3886
18thcatelier.com

embroidery palace
Los Angeles, California
(310) 273-8003
floriocollection.com

fanciful designs
San Clemente, California
etsy.com/shop/FancifulDesign

french basketeer
Laguna Beach, California
(949) 310-5687
frenchbasketeer.com

frenchblue & co.
San Clemente, California
(949) 291-5714
frenchblueandco.com

french garden house
Huntington Beach, California
(714) 454-3231
frenchgardenhouse.com

full bloom cottage
Orange, California
(714) 600-8971
fullbloomcottage.com

william haines designs
West Hollywood, California
(310) 289-0280
williamhaines.com

halsea
Newport Beach, California
halsea.com

hearts desire interior design
(949) 637-1233

house inc.
Santa Monica, California
(310) 449-1918
annettetatum.com

les indiennes
Germantown, New York
(518) 537-3735
lesindiennesshop.com

one kings lane
onekingslane.com

paris hotel boutique
San Francisco, California
(415) 305-7846
parishotelboutique.com

john robshaw textiles
New York, New York
(212) 594-6006
johnrobshaw.com

st. barths home
Laguna Beach, California
(800) 274-9096
stbarthshome.com

thurston/boyd interior design
Laguna Beach, California
(949) 376-0477
thurstonboyd.com

tumbleweed & dandelion
Venice, California
(310) 450-4310
tumbleweedanddandelion.com

velvet & linen/giannetti home
Los Angeles, California
(310) 820-1329
giannettiarchitects.com

vintageweave interiors, inc.
Los Angeles, California
(323) 932-0451
vintageweave.com

baroness monica von neumann
Los Angeles, California
baronessmonicavonneumann.com

maude woods
Pasadena, California
(626) 577-3400
maudewoods.com

acknowledgments

To Luc and Allan Rosen, the two men in my life who can barge in on my space anytime. Well, perhaps after knocking.

To Aliza Fogelson, Angelin Borsics, Ashley Tucker, Amy Sly, Stephanie Huntwork, Patricia Shaw, Eleanor Jackson, Bridgett Hurley, Erin Lang Masercola, Elena Oh, Jickie Torres, Hillary Black, Meryl Schoenbaum, Rebecca Ittner, Marisa Crawford, Bret Gum, Jaimee Itagaki, and Mark Tanner.

The homeowners: Lidy Baars, Sally Bartz, Randy Boyd, Carrie and Marty Davitch, Kathleen Delgado, Clara DiGiuseppe, Yvette Dobbie, Susan Ellison, Susan Feldman, Brooke Giannetti, Lynn Goldfinger, Loretta Kilheffer, Donald Kirkby, Lizzie McGraw, Ann Millang, Susie Mitchell, Janet Rodriguez, Janet Solomon, Noel Solomon, Maria Tam, Annette Tatum, Michelle Tingler, Natalie Umbert, and Baroness Monica von Neumann.

Many thanks to green tea and gardenia candles, the trusted pair that helped me through a few long nights.

index